Living The Life Of Faith

LIVING THE LIFE OF FAITH

Henry Byamukama (AP)

LAURUS BOOKS

Unless otherwise notated, all Scripture references are from the New King James Version®. Copyright © 1982 by Thomas Nelson, Inc. Used by permission. All rights reserved.

Scriptures quotations marked KJV are from the King James Version of the Holy Bible, available in the Public Domain.

LIVING THE LIFE OF FAITH

By Henry Byamukama (AP)

Copyright © 2022 by Henry Byamukama (AP)

All rights reserved. This book is protected under the copyright laws of the United States of America. This book may not be copied or reprinted for commercial gain or profit. The use of short quotations or occasional page copying for personal or group study is permitted and encouraged. Permission will be granted on request.

Paperback: ISBN: 978-1-943523-90-0
Mobi (Kindle): ISBN: 978-1-943523-91-7
ePub (iBooks, Nook): 978-1-943523-92-4

Published by LAURUS BOOKS

LAURUS BOOKS
A DIVISION OF THE LAURUS COMPANY, INC.
www.TheLaurusCompany.com

This book may be purchased in paperback from:
www.TheLaurusCompany.com, Amazon.com, and other retailers around the world. May also be available in formats for electronic readers from their respective stores. Available to booksellers at Spring Arbor.

DEDICATION

Dear Reader,

I feel great joy knowing that I am able to hold a conversation with you through this book. As you delve deeper, my prayer is that you will be sensitive to hear the Holy Spirit as He speaks to you through it and that your faith is strengthened.

This book is especially dedicated to you.

—Henry Byamukama

ACKNOWLEDGEMENTS

I would like, first of all, to thank my wife Lillian for 15 years of marriage, and my two children, Hadassah and Corban. Thank you for your patience, strength, and support always.

To Rev. Nancy E. Williams, President of The Laurus Company, Inc. Your friendship is invaluable. Thank you for all of the support that you render me. It is highly appreciated.

Special thanks to Eseza Nabaggala for all of your editorial work.

Above all, I thank the Holy Spirit, my constant Helper, for all of the wisdom and direction He always gives me.

TABLE OF CONTENTS

Dedication 5
Acknowledgements 7
Preface 11
Introduction 13

Chapter One
Faith is The Foundation 17

Chapter Two
Faith and The New You 25

Chapter Three
Faith and Grace 37

Chapter Four
Faith and The Word 49

Chapter Five
Faith and Your Thoughts 61

Chapter Six
Faith and Prayer 67

Chapter Seven
Possessing and Contending Aspects of Faith 75

Chapter Eight
Faith is of The Now 85

Chapter Nine
Let Faith Be Your Definition 93

Conclusion 101
A Call to Salvation 105
About the Author 109

Preface

*I tell you that He will avenge them speedily.
Nevertheless, when the Son of Man comes, will He
really find faith on the earth?* – Luke 18:8

In my ministry life, I have experienced transition in message and operation over the years. In the last few years, the message of faith has been paramount in my spirit. It is the reason behind the authorship of this manuscript.

Faith is variant. Hebrews 11:4-40 is an account of faith. If we were to do research and ask Abraham, "What is faith?" he would most probably say that faith is when God calls you out of your country to a land that He will show you. Noah would probably say faith is building an ark for God. Enoch would probably say that faith is walking with God until you are translated. Abel would probably say that faith is offering a more excellent sacrifice than Cain. Each of the Patriarchs would define faith according to their own experience with God.

Question: *What is faith?* Each and every one of us has our own definition according to our unique experiences with

God. Without a doubt, every single human being is divinely unique. There are no duplicates, according to divine design.

As you delve into this writing, my prayer is that your eyes will be opened to receive a fresh revelation of faith, that you may be shaped according to God's design, and that you may be able to manifest your peculiarity.

INTRODUCTION

Faith is Predictable

For by it [faith] *the elders obtained a good report.*
– Hebrews 11:2 (bracketed words added)

*I would have lost heart, unless I had BELIEVED that I would see the goodness of the L*ORD *in the land of the living.*
– Psalm 27:13 (emphasis added)

Where is boasting then? It is excluded. By what law? Of works? No, but by the law of faith.
– Romans 3:27

Faith is the human response to divinity. God has prescribed a lifestyle by which the justified should live. See this in Hebrews 10:38: *Now the just shall live by faith...* It is spiritual in nature. It is not mental; it defies logic. It cannot be measured empirically. It is results oriented. It comes by hearing. It is potent. And it is in the now.

There is a hearing of faith, a talk of faith, a walk of faith, a prayer of faith, and an action of faith tantamount to a faith life!

There are laws set in place in a country, home, or organization. Not heeding to these laws has consequences. If you park wrongly, your car gets booted. When you commit a crime, you get prosecuted and judged accordingly.

The human being without spiritual guidance and support is like a tree with shallow roots.

> ***For God so loved the world that he gave his only begotten Son, that whosoever believeth in Him should not perish but have everlasting life.*** – John 3:16

When you believe, you receive. You believe, you will be saved. You believe, you will be healed.

The law of faith is this: when you believe, you receive. Period!

CHAPTER ONE

Faith is the Foundation

Now faith is the substance [foundation] *of things hoped for, the evidence of things not seen.*
– Hebrews 11:1 (Bracketed word added)

This Scripture could as well read: "Faith is the foundation of the things that we hope for, the evidence of things not seen." If faith is the foundation of what we hope for, what is the foundation of faith? The foundation of our faith is the Word of God!

Believing does not come from seeing. We cannot build our belief upon miracles. Rather, miracles are a byproduct of our believing. We do not believe because we have seen miracles. Miracles do not bring faith. Rather, faith brings miracles.

> *But also for this very reason, giving all diligence, add to your faith virtue, to virtue knowledge …* – 2 Peter 1:5

It is of great importance that whatever we do, it is built on the rock. Without this foundation, the ground is shaky.

> *But he who doubts is condemned if he eats, because he does*

not eat from faith; for whatever is not from faith is sin.
– Romans 14:23

It is a sin to doubt God with all the wonderful promises He has given us in His Word and how He has explained the authority that He has over all the heavens and the earth. It surely should displease Him every time we choose not to take Him at His word.

It is only by faith that we please God. God is moved by our faith in His Word and His integrity. He is not moved by our fasting, making loud prayers, and doing great deeds. As much as all of these things are important and should be done, if done without faith, they are done in futility.

Faith comes by hearing

So then faith comes by hearing, and hearing by the word of God. – Romans 10:17

The reason many Christians fail is because they are not discipled into a strong faith foundation based on the Word of God. You cannot have genuine working faith without hearing the voice of God. It is possible to hear a good preaching and not hear God. Why? It is because the voice of God is a spiritual voice.

Therefore He who supplies the Spirit to you and works miracles among you, does He do it by the works of the law, or by the hearing of faith? – Galatians 3:5

Faith comes by hearing, _and_ hearing BY the Word of God.

Everything you hear must be judged by the Word of God. Each time you hear the Word, you hear God speak. Then you know God's thinking pattern.

Faith guarantees victory. Impossibility is not faith vocabulary. It is better that you die believing than you die doubting.

In 1998, God spoke to me to go into full-time ministry. I had no Bible training, no financial support, and no church backing me up. But because of the clarity of the voice of God and His persuasion, I stepped out in faith, and my faith has produced results. Twenty years later, God has used me in ways I could not have fathomed He would. I have come to learn and believe that when God speaks, He provides.

The voice of God in our inner being never makes sense, and it is not meant to. The voice of God is meant to make faith. God tells Abraham to go out of his country to a place that he neither knew nor had ever heard of. Abraham obeyed and went. We all know how his story ended; it ended in victory.

> *Declare this:*
> **My tomorrow is secure in Jesus' name.**

Be careful what you hear and how you hear

If you abide in Me, and My words abide in you, you will ask what you desire, and it shall be done for you. – John 15:7

There are many voices: soulish, circumstantial, and reason. Important to note is that if we don't build up our inner man, our inner being gets clouded with other voices.

Therefore we do not lose heart. Even though our outward man is perishing, yet the inward man is being renewed day by day. – 2 Corinthians

Not so many years ago, a friend of mine was directed by God to take some time to pray and fast. The instruction was that she was to spend time with God at her home. However, in the middle of the day, she thought she should move out to attend to some pressing issues at work. We encouraged her not to go, but she was adamant and went. Sadly, on her way back home, she was shot dead. Had she listened and acted on the instruction of God, and not listened to and followed her soulish voice, she would be alive today.

We build up our inner man by praying in the Spirit. Jude urges us:

But you, beloved, building yourselves up on your most holy faith, praying in the Holy Spirit ... – Jude 1:20

By this, you build your inner man day by day. It is possible to be affected by the Word of God—spirit, soul, and body.

For the word of God is living and powerful, and sharper than any two-edged sword, piercing even to the division of soul

and spirit, and of joints and marrow, and is a discerner of the thoughts and intents of the heart.
— Hebrews 4:12

Revelation brings light. The hearing of faith causes an enlightenment in the inner being.

The entrance of your words gives light; it gives understanding to the simple. — Psalm 119:130

... the eyes of your understanding being enlightened; that you may know what is the hope of His calling, what are the riches of the glory of His inheritance in the saints ...
— Ephesians 1:18

The same is true with doubt. Doubt and uncertainty also come by hearing, and hearing by the word of fear.

And they gave the children of Israel a bad report of the land which they had spied out, saying, "The land through which we have gone as spies is a land that devours its inhabitants, and all the people whom we saw in it are men of great stature.
— Numbers 13:32

The ten spies gave an evil report of the land that they had gone to spy. It was such an evil report that they almost stoned Joshua and Caleb who tried to speak faith to them, by giving them a better report that the inhabitants of the land of Canaan were actually bread for the Israelites.

Even when they reminded them that God was with them and they need not fear, the Israelites would have none of it. They forgot all the miracles that God had performed for them. The parting of the Red Sea, the provision of water from a rock, the provision of manna, the pillar of fire at night, and the dark cloud during day.

They chose to dwell on the fear in their hearts. God was so displeased with them that apart from Joshua and Caleb, none of the people in that generation from twenty years old and upwards ever made it to the promised land of Canaan.

Be careful what you hear and how you hear. Faith is based on the Word of God, and the Word of God only. Positive confession does not bring faith, though it is necessary in faith building, but rather it builds hope. And hope deferred makes the heart sick (see Proverbs 13:12).

CHAPTER TWO

Faith and The New You

For God so loved the world that He gave His only begotten Son, that whosoever believes in Him should not perish but have everlasting life. – John 3:16

When we heard the Word of God, we responded through faith and believed in the Savior, Jesus Christ. This is the faith that drew us to God through faith unto salvation, the response to the gospel that was preached to us through salvation. In this, faith was birthed, and we responded.

But what does it say? "The word is near you, in your mouth and in your heart" (that is, the word of faith which we preach): that if you confess with your mouth the Lord Jesus and believe in your heart that God has raised Him from the dead, you will be saved. – Romans 10:8-9

Faith is in our hearts and our mouths. Isn't it such an amazing thing that in order to be saved, all we need is to believe the Word of God? There are no twelve steps and no terrifying rituals that we have to undergo.

As we listen to the word of faith preached, the Holy Spirit convicts our hearts to confession, and the result is salvation.

What happens when we are born again?

Nicodemus said to Him, "How can a man be born when he is old? Can he enter a second time into his mother's womb and be born?" – John 3:4

In verse 6, Jesus explains to Nicodemus: *That which is born of the flesh is flesh, and that which is born of the Spirit is spirit.*

We have a natural birth (being born of the flesh) and a spiritual birth (being born of the Spirit as a result of salvation).

When we are born again, our spirit man is recreated. When you accept Christ as your Lord and Savior, it is your spirit that is born again into the nature and likeness of God. It is not your eyes or nose that gets born again. It is your spirit. This is why you still look the same physically as you did before you were born again.

The life, ability, and nature of God is imparted into our spirit. God is Spirit, and you contact Him spiritually.

But as many as received Him, to them He gave the right to become children of God, to those who believe in His name:
– John 1:12

We also received the gift of faith.

For by grace you have been saved through faith, and that not of yourselves; it is the gift of God, … – Ephesians 2:8

> **But the fruit of the Spirit is love, joy, peace, longsuffering, kindness, goodness, faithfulness ...** – Galatians 5:22

It is upon this gift of faith (in seed form in our inner being) that we build, thus bearing fruit. This fruit is a result of the Word sowed in our inner man. This is the kind that works with us to walk the faith walk; faith that is a result of the continuous sowing of the seed (Word) into our spirits.

> *"Listen! Behold, a sower went out to sow ... And He said, "The kingdom of God is as if a man should scatter seed on the ground ...* – Mark 4:3, 26

In the new creation, the Kingdom is all about sowing the seed (the Word), watering it, and the seed (the Word) bringing forth fruit. In the new creation, we have faith that is a result of the planted seed (the Word). We receive salvation by faith, we fight the good fight of faith, and we overcome this world by faith.

Eternal life is received

> *... that whoever believes in Him should not perish but have eternal life.* – John 3:15

Eternal life is already in your heart at salvation. Fear waits by the door to take hold of our hearts. The moment fear gains access, progress is halted—spirit, soul, and body. When the Word of God is not implanted in your spirit or revealed to you, fear is planted. When fear is planted in our inner beings, even the spiritual rivers will be hindered from consistent flow. Faith is more than seeking. It attracts and bears fruit.

We are God's representation on the earth because earth is an extension of heaven (delegated authority)

> *The heaven, even the heavens, are the LORD's; but the earth He has given to the children of men.* – Psalm 115:16

> *Then the dust will return to the earth as it was, and the spirit will return to God who gave it.* – Ecclesiastes 12:7

Eternal life means that our spirits are alive and in sync with the Spirit of God, and when we die, we (our spirits) will go to heaven. A spirit that has not been recreated is dead, and it cannot coexist with God's Spirit. When we die, our spirits will return back to God, and our bodies will rot in the ground. The body is meant to perish. When you die, your inner man returns to God because your body can no longer contain it.

> *But there is a spirit in man, and the breath of the Almighty gives him understanding.* – Job 32:8

The power for rulership, guidance, direction, and innovation has been given to man. God's way is partnership. We are co-workers with God. God's Spirit bears witness with my spirit in order to establish the Kingdom.

> *The spirit of a man is the lamp of the LORD, searching all the inner depths of his heart.* – Proverbs 20:27

Jesus said, "My meat is to do the will of Him who sent me." He also said He would not do anything except what He saw the Father do. The price for knowing the will of God is doing it and completing it.

The connection between being born again and faith

When you become born again, that man (the spirit man) is a new creature, but he is a baby and has to be trained how to live by faith. The spirit man in you is so powerful. The real you (your spirit) can't be seen. That is why when you do certain things, people can't understand how you did them because we understand mostly by our senses. The best prophet to yourself is you.

> *Put this book down for a minute and prophesy to yourself.*
> *Speak what you want to see in your life.*
> *You don't need to wait for anybody to tell you for you to feel good.*
> *All you need is to speak by faith.*
> *What you say to yourself is so important.*

Therefore we do not lose heart. Even though our outward man is perishing, yet the inward man is being renewed day by day. – 2 Corinthians 4:16

The human being is the only spirit that has legal authority to function on this earth. For any spirit to function, it must be embodied. God is the Creator; you are the created. Your divine responsibility is to hear His will and to do it. God responds to us in accordance with His will. In other words, God is only obligated to answer His Word.

> ***Keep your heart with all diligence, for out of it spring the issues of life.*** – Proverbs 4:23

The heart spoken of here is not your blood-pumping system. It is your spiritual nature where God dwells.

You are a spirit. This is why when you die, your spirit gets out of your body and goes to God.

Feed your spirit on spiritual food

> ***But He answered and said, "It is written, 'Man shall not live by bread alone, but by every word that proceeds from the mouth of God.'"*** – Matthew 4:4

Man is a spirit, and he feeds on spiritual food. The spiritual foods on which our spirits live are the Word of God, worship of God, and prayer.

Just like we may have health deficiencies, it is possible to have spiritual deficiencies. Every time we neglect to feed our spirits, the growth of the inward man is stunted and malnourished. It is at such moments that we are unable to put our faith to work.

For us to produce good fruit, we need to keep sowing the Word of God into our spirits.

> ***"... But these are the ones sown on good ground, those who hear the word, accept it, and bear fruit: some thirtyfold, some sixty, and some a hundred."*** – Mark 4:20

You cannot harvest what you have not sown. Faith is a product of your inner man state, how taught it is, how it is fed. You cannot get supernatural results by natural means. Religion talks about going to heaven. Faith talks about heaven coming to you.

Religion is man's interpretation of God. Revelation is God illuminating man's inner being. I have been to places where ten men have had to share one Bible, but those ten men had stronger faith than men who have their own personal copies of the Bible, along with other Bible translations, Bible concordances, and Bible dictionaries.

The Bible says that the world is held by the word of His power. God is raising up a faith generation that is going to take over the world. The Kingdom of God system is different from the world system. The Kingdom of God system is in control. If all the preachers in the world stopped preaching, the world would collapse.

It is possible to be full of faith and power. Stephen is an excellent example for us to look at.

> ***And Stephen, full of faith and power, did great wonders and signs among the people.*** – Acts 6:8

With faith comes the power to do exceedingly above all that we have ever imagined. So we therefore understand that it is impossible to have spiritual growth without faith growth.

This faith can also be seen. When you look at some people, you see fear. In others, you see the radiance of the belief that there is One who is higher than every circumstance, higher than all flesh and blood.

> *When Jesus saw their faith, He said to the paralytic, "Son, your sins are forgiven you."* – Mark 2:5

True worship for the children of God

> *But the hour is coming, and now is, when the true worshipers will worship the Father in spirit and truth; for the Father is seeking such to worship Him. God is Spirit, and those who worship Him must worship in spirit and truth."*
> – John 4:23-24

Jesus was explaining to the Samaritan woman He met at the well that a time would come when we would not have a specific location to go to in order to worship God because salvation would open up another dimension.

It is impossible to know God naturally. The natural man is incapable of knowing God because God can only be known spiritually. It is impossible to worship God if it is not done spiritually.

The faith force is a spirit force. God can only be contacted spiritually. The spiritual realm is more real than the material realm. Spiritual things only respond to spiritual people. This is the reason why you cannot shoot a demon using a bullet. Every time you worship, you glorify God.

Worshiping God also guarantees that we shall have the victory. King Jehoshaphat, Paul, and Silas were victorious because they chose to worship instead of being fearful.

> *And Jehoshaphat bowed his head with his face to the ground,*

and all Judah and the inhabitants of Jerusalem bowed before the LORD, worshipping the LORD. ... Now when they began to sing and to praise, the LORD set ambushes against the people of Ammon, Moab, and Mount Seir, who had come against Judah; and they were defeated.
– 2 Chronicles 20:18, 22

But at midnight Paul and Silas were praying and singing hymns to God, and the prisoners were listening to them. Suddenly there was a great earthquake, so that the foundations of the prison were shaken; and immediately all the doors were opened and everyone's chains were loosed. – Acts 16:25-26

Faith through worship will produce tremendous results in your life in ways that you cannot comprehend. Stop worrying about what tomorrow brings, and put your praise garments on.

Sanctified for His good pleasure

There is therefore now no condemnation to those who are in Christ Jesus, who do not walk according to the flesh, but according to the Spirit. – Romans 8:1

Because of condemnation and the sin consciousness, man has a limitation in approaching God. This condemnation robs us of faith in the workings of God. It keeps us in bondage to fear. The condemnation also causes us not to feel good enough to pray or to deserve an answer to prayer.

Condemnation causes us to keep away from the subject of God. Guilty consciences give birth to philosophies of men that lead to the killing of our faith. This is why it is important for us to know what we are in Christ and its availability.

When you get born again, you are set aside for the work of God. You are able to communicate with God, Spirit to spirit. He is able to direct you, correct you, and you can clearly hear Him as He speaks.

... for it is God who works in you both to will and to do for His good pleasure. – Philippians 2:13

When I believe, my heart changes, and my changed heart produces the right actions. It is not the actions that produce the changed heart.

Religion says that for you to see God, you need to clean your heart. Faith says sanctify it, cleansing it with the washing of water through the Word.

... that He might sanctify and cleanse her with the washing of water by the word ... – Ephesians 5:26

When this word comes to you, it cannot leave you the same. Faith is not judicial. It is not what you deserve that you get. It is what you believe you get. You do not have to defend yourself. Stop trusting in your goodness, and start trusting in God's goodness.

As you therefore have received Christ Jesus the Lord, so walk in Him ... – Colossians 2:6

For your faith to operate maximally, you must operate in spiritual activity because faith is spiritual. You must engage in spiritual activity by praying in tongues and making spiritual declarations.

CHAPTER THREE

Faith and Grace

The *Strong's Concordance Lite** describes **_grace_** as *the merciful kindness by which God, exerting His holy influence upon souls, turns them to Christ, keeps, strengthens, increases them in Christian faith, knowledge, affection, and kindles them to the exercises of the Christian virtues.*

Saved by grace through faith

Whatever is of grace is by faith. Grace is God's response to my predicament. Faith is my response to God's response. We are saved by faith through the grace of God. Grace is everything that Christ did that I could not do. We respond to the grace of God spiritually and not carnally. Everything that was provided for by Christ we receive it by faith. We believe God

---
*Copyright © Orion Systems 2010-2017

by faith, and we obtain a good report by faith.

> ***We then, as workers together with Him also plead with you not to receive the grace of God in vain.*** – 2 Corinthians 6:1

You receive the grace of God in vain if your faith does not meet with grace; or simply put, you receive the grace of God in vain when it is not connected to faith. Faith is the divine response to the grace of God. Faith responds to grace.

It is by faith that we confess Jesus as our Lord and Savior. What we oftentimes fail to understand is that at that moment, there is a divine exchange. Your sinful nature is exchanged for the blood that Jesus shed at the Cross. There is therefore no longer any need for us to strive for self-righteousness.

> ***And of his fullness we have all received, and grace for grace.***
> – John 1:16

We receive grace out of the only One who can handle us. It is not our actions that determine our righteousness. Our righteousness is filthiness to God. We are only the righteousness of God. When we were born again, we were made right the moment we believed. When we believed, God in us produced actions that made us right. The grace of God keeps and sustains us in our Christian walk.

Revelation in the complete work of Christ

> ***For the law of the Spirit of life in Christ Jesus has made me free from the law of sin and death.*** – Romans 8:2

Man's need, physical and spiritual, was completely dealt with at redemption. Because of Christ, man can stand complete in Christ; He has partaken in the fullness of God.

> *... being justified freely by His grace through the redemption that is in Christ Jesus ...* – Romans 3:24

Redemption is real, and we have been redeemed from the curse of the law (sin, sickness and disease, death, and poverty). We are also redeemed from darkness to light and into freedom. We are established in favor, calling, and established in grace. Our position in Christ and our fellowship that we lost is restored.

> *... through whom also we have access by faith into this grace in which we stand, and rejoice in hope of the glory of God.*
> – Romans 5:2

We stand in grace. We walk by faith.

The just live by faith

> *For in it the righteousness of God is revealed from faith to faith; as it is written, "The just shall live by faith."*
> – Romans 1:17

Now that we have been justified, the commended way for us to live is by faith.

When we accepted Jesus as Lord and Savior of our lives, we also received the measure of faith.

> *For I say, through the grace given unto me, to every man that*

> *is among you, not to think of himself more highly than he ought to think; but to think soberly, according as God hath dealt to every man THE MEASURE OF FAITH.*
> – Romans 12:3 KJV (emphasis added)

The word "the" is a definite article, which calls to our attention that the measure of faith given to us is certain. Every believer has faith, but this measure of faith can be multiplied. Our faith is based on the Word of God. The more revelation of the Word that we have in our spirit, the more our faith grows. And every time we exercise our faith, it increases. You cannot believe God for 100 million before you have believed Him for 10 million.

> *Simon Peter, a servant and an apostle of Jesus Christ, to them that have obtained like precious faith with us through the righteousness of God and our Savior Jesus Christ.*
> – 2 Peter 1:1 KJV

We all receive the same faith, the spiritual ability to respond to what God has said. It is not mental. It is not cram work. Some people cram the Bible and are still dead. Let the Word of God flow in you. Religion kills. Faith flows; it is a river of living water. Where faith is concerned, you cannot become worse. You will only become better.

Speak forth the word

Faith operates through saying, and continuously saying, the Word of God. God created the worlds by speaking. He said, *"Let there be,"* and all kinds of creation came into being. He has given us the same power with our tongue. He tells us:

Let the redeemed of the LORD SAY SO, Whom He has redeemed from the hand of the enemy.
– Psalms 107:2 (emphasis added)

> **Now declare. "I am blessed and highly favored. I am blessed beyond a curse, in Jesus' name."**

As a child of God, authoritative declaration is paramount.

Thou shalt also decree a thing, and it shall be established unto thee: and the light shall shine upon thy ways. – Job 22:28

Death and life are in the power of the tongue: and they that love it shall eat the fruit thereof. – Proverbs 18:21

We have a creative force within us. With the tongue, we either kill or give life to something. Whatever you say will most definitely come to pass. Faith works with decreeing power.

I believed, therefore have I spoken: ... – Psalm 116:10

Faith is a spiritual force, it comes by hearing. I believe because God said. After you have heard and believed, the next thing to do is to speak and declare the Word of God; to yourself, your family, your ministry, your academics and every obstacle seemingly standing in your way.

... if ye have faith as a grain of a mustard seed, ye shall say unto this mountain, Remove hence to yonder place; and it

shall remove; and nothing shall be impossible unto you.
– Matthew 17:20 KJV

Paul had the same source of faith as the Psalmist, and the source where this faith came from necessitates declaration.

Faith is dependent on the word in your spirit

It is the spirit that quickeneth; the flesh profiteth nothing: the words that I speak unto you, they are spirit, and they are life.
– John 6:63 KJV

God is Spirit. He does not speak in the realm of knowledge; He speaks in your innermost being. As He communicates to your spirit, it is like a seed that is planted in the ground. The growth begins from under the ground, and the plant sprouts through into a flower, a tree, or any other kind of plant.

Likewise, as the Spirit of God communicates to our spirits through the Word; growth begins from the inside and manifests outwardly. Faith grows in your spirit, and the results of your faith show in the physical.

Your faith is dependent on the amount of seed (Word) that has been plantedin your spirit. No seed, no fruit (faith). Little seed, little fruit (faith). Much seed, much fruit (faith). It is the same principle applied in a farm. You cannot plant two acres of a crop and expect to reap eight acres of harvest. You cannot fake faith. You cannot figure it out. It is a fruit. It grows naturally.

As you read on, faith is coming to you, and you will realize that what was impossible has been demystified because faith comes and comes. Something is happening in your belly right now, and by the end of this book, you will realize that no single situation that you were finding impossible is standing before you. Hallelujah!

We are the righteousness of God

But we are all like an unclean thing, and all our righteousnesses are as filthy rags; we all fade as a leaf; and our iniquities, like the wind, have taken us away. – Isaiah 64:6

The righteousness of God ensures that because of what He has done for me, anytime, I can stand before God any moment, without guilt, fear, and condemnation because I understand that the blood of Jesus is enough.

Let us therefore come boldly to the throne of grace, that we may obtain mercy and find grace to help in time of need.
– Hebrews 4:16

The part in me that looks like God is my spirit man. It is impossible for you to have genuine rest unless you make spiritual contact because you are connecting with your righteousness. Unless you make spiritual contact, you will search forever. The knowledge of God is not mental, it is a spiritual knowledge.

You know it not because you are educated, but because you have made contact with the Spirit. The real you can never be satisfied from your sensual faculties. You cannot satisfy yourself sensually because genuine joy comes from God into your spirit. Your mind, emotions, and sight are sensual. You cannot get the genuine peace and joy from your senses.

> *Peace I leave with you, My peace I give to you, not as the world gives do I give to you. Let not your heart be troubled, neither let it be afraid.* – John 14:27

Sin is no longer in control

We all know what sin is. What we may not know is that when we were born again, we became the righteousness of God. Something that is more powerful took over our lives. Sin is no longer in control; it is the inner man under the subjection of the Spirit who is now in control.

It is important to know how the righteousness of God and the faith of God are available to us. It is only through redemption that God meets every need of the human. The human being is the only one that has a spiritual need, an emotional need, an intellectual need, and a physical need. Money can meet your needs apart from the spiritual need. Only God has the complete package.

> *Abstain from all appearance of evil. And the very God of peace sanctify you wholly; and I pray God your whole spirit and soul and body be preserved blameless unto the coming of our Lord Jesus Christ.* – 1 Thessalonians 5:22-23 KJV

When you accept Jesus as your Savior, your spirit is born again; your soul (mind, will, emotions) is not. Your mind can't be born again; it can only be transformed by the renewing of your mind by the implanted Word of God. (See

Romans 12:2.)

The believer at salvation is a partaker of the fullness of Christ, which is a supernaturally impartation. Even when the mind does not understand what is happening, the spirit has already received. This is where faith comes in.

CHAPTER FOUR

Faith and The Word of God

Faith is the faithful application of what God has said. The Word of God is meant to make faith. Faith is not a theological argument; faith flows. The word that we preach must be mixed with faith if it is to profit.

Through faith we understand that the worlds were framed by the word of God, so that things which are seen were not made of things which do appear. – Hebrews 11:3 KJV

In the beginning, God spoke, and everything came into being. By His word, the world was created. Everything happening in your life has a spiritual foundation.

It is mandatory for us to conform to the Word of God and not the other way round. The full manifestation of the Word of God is heaven on earth. There is nothing as sure as faith based on the Word of God. We can bet every last penny we have that God will come through with what He has said to us through His Word.

The Word is eternal

The grass withers, the flower fades, but the word of our God stands forever. – Isaiah 40:8

Everything will pass away. All that we hold dear for ourselves will one day be no more, but the Word of God will endure through all the seasons, fashions, fads, and generations. So matter what we may be going through, we have the assurance of the Word of God that it is but for a moment. As long as we remain in the faith, then we shall triumph.

Having hope is not the same as having faith. Hope is based on positive confession; faith is based on the Word of God. You believe it because God said it. We can always bank on the integrity of God.

Through faith we understand that the worlds were framed by the word of God, so that things which are seen were not made of things which do appear – Hebrews 11:3 KJV

We believe because God said. There should be no other reason. Through what God says, we understand why things are the way they are. The spiritual realm is the mother realm. When you see fruit in your life, it means that there is something in the root. Faith deals with your issue from the root.

And in the morning, as they passed by, they saw the fig tree dried up from the roots. – Mark 11:20 KJV

God tackles our issues from the root. Faith is not struggling, it is flowing. You don't prove a point to anybody. Your anointing is so unique; there is no one like you.

Faith always triumphs

For our light affliction, which is but for a moment, is working for us a far more exceeding and eternal weight of glory.
– 2 Corinthians 4:17

Faith dictates your season and your time. How are season and time understood? They are understood by faith. You don't have to wait for a certain geographical time. Every created thing is subject to time because God created day and night. In the beginning, *God said, "Let there be light"; and there was light. ... and God divided the light from the darkness. God called the light Day, and the darkness He called Night. So the evening and the morning were the first day.* (Genesis 1:3-5). So He created time and seasons.

Why man is subject to time and why he is a slave of deadlines is an indication that something is wrong. Only faith will bypass those kinds of deadlines. If it is created, then it is subject to change.

We are not limited by age or location; the only thing that limits us is if our faith is not put to work. Let there be a generation rising that is limitless, and nothing shall put us down.

One time, I was preaching in China, and in the middle of my sermon, the interpreter suddenly left the pulpit. The congregation could neither understand English nor my local dialect.

The only way for me to communicate was in Chinese, and I could only speak a few Chinese words. These Chinese were spiritual people like me, and all I needed was to communicate in my spiritual language, so I began to communicate in tongues, and miracles started happening.

Faith is of the Spirit

And the Lord said, "Simon, Simon! Indeed, Satan has asked for you, that he may sift you as wheat. But I have prayed for you, that your faith should not fail; and when you have returned to Me, strengthen your brethren." – Luke 22:31-32

Faith is not taking a blind leap. Though we cannot measure it in a laboratory, it is measured spiritually. But it is not walking blindly. It is walking to "thus says the Lord." It cannot be tested sensually because it supersedes the sensual realm. It is of the Spirit.

The Spirit and the word agree all the time. There are no contradictions between them. The Elders obtained good reports, under different circumstances and space of time. The common factor was faith. Faith is what gives you understanding into the spiritual world. It is faith that determines the things I see.

The Word is the truth

The life of faith will ultimately have an effect on the realm of

Chapter 4: Faith and The Word of God

truth and the realm of fact, ensuring that you have the last laugh.

And you shall know the truth, and the truth shall make you free. - John 8:32

The truth is spiritual realities. This means that truth is how it has been established in the realm of the Spirit. How has God established that specific principle in the Spirit? This is what Jesus came to usher us into, so that we can see how that specific aspect is established in the Spirit.

*And Elisha prayed, and said, "L*ORD*, I pray, open his eyes, that he may see." Then the L*ORD *opened the eyes of the young man, and he saw. And, behold, the mountain was full of horses and chariots of fire all around Elisha.*
– 2 Kings 6:17

Every natural fact is subject to a spiritual truth. The horses surrounding the city are a fact. The realm of truth is simply spiritual activity that surrounds the personality of Jesus that has been established. You can't change the fact that by His stripes you were healed.

The servant's response was because of lack understanding. Elisha's response was that the eyes of the servant's be opened. This is because he needed to understand. Faith sees to the end, the bible says you shall end well. It doesn't end at your now; facts are eventually worn down, if you persevere in faith.

Truth that is consistently applied will eventually wear out the natural facts. The truth that by His stripes we were healed consistently applied wears out the physical ailment. So many years ago I fell sick to a point of death because of the pain in my chest. I declared health to my body until the pain disappeared and I was totally healed.

We perish by lack of knowledge

My people are destroyed for lack of knowledge: because you have rejected knowledge, I will also reject you, that you shall be no priest to me: because you have forgotten the law of your God, I will also forget your children. –Hosea 4:6

The greatest enemy of our faith growth is the lack of understanding of God's word. Your faith can't grow beyond your knowledge of God's word. When your understanding of God's word grows, your faith grows. When your faith is not growing, it means that you have substituted revelation for growth.

We perish by lack of spiritual knowledge. A carnal person is one who walks by what he sees, tastes, touches, feels and hears. A carnal Christian is a perverse Christian. Perversion is anything that is not of faith.

When you don't have knowledge, (knowing God intimately from your inner being), you begin to operate in religion, trying to please God. You can't love God; God loved you so much that He sent Jesus to die on the Cross for our sins. We love God because He loved us.

And hope makes not ashamed; because the love of God is shed abroad in our hearts by the Holy Spirit who is given unto us.
– Romans 5:5

The Spirit in us causes us to love God. It causes us to be sold out in our service to Him and to minister to Him with everything that we have got.

Faith calls those things which are not, as though they were

(As it is written, I have made you a father of many nations,) before him whom he believed, even God, who gives life to the dead, and calls those things which are not as though they were. – Romans 4:16-17

Life should not be dependent on what others say or your qualifications, but on what God said. Your life is not a sum total of your mistakes, it is a sum total of what God said. Everyone always has an opinion about you.

The newspaper, magazines and celebrities are constantly setting standards for which most of us don't qualify. If you start to consider them, then you turn your eyes off of God. Then Like Lot's wife, you turn into a pillar of salt, seeking to attain such standards as you shouldn't because they are not in line with your call or purpose on earth.

God is a faith God; you should be a faith man. The abode of our faith is from the spirit.

But the Lord said unto Samuel, Look not on his countenance, or on the height of his stature; because I have refused him: for the Lord sees not as man sees; for man looks on the outward appearance, but the Lord looks on the heart.
– 1 Samuel 16:7

Man looks on the natural things; God looks on the eternal things. Heart is the same as spirit of a man or inner being. Man deals on what he can see, on the dimension of what he has been exposed to. It is a temporary value, but God sees those things which are eternal.

While man can write you off as a failure, God sees the treasure in you, and surely, at the fullness of time, the rest of the world will see that treasure. In the book, **God's Generals**, by Robert Liardon, he writes about great men and women who did such exploits to God. However, some were men whom the world had cast off because no one thought anything great would become of them. Some were illiterate, others were drunkards. Mariah Woodworth-Etter lost five of her six children, and yet God chose and used each of them in tremendous ways.

Bearing fruit as a result of abiding in the Word of God

> *I am the vine, you are the branches. He who abides in Me, and I in him, bears much fruit; for without Me you can do nothing.* – John 15:5

Bearing fruit is a result of the Word of God abiding in you. Any time spent in reading and studying the Word of God is not a waste. The Spirit causes the Word of God to rub with your spirit, and hence, you begin to bear fruit in all areas of your life.

This is how miracles begin to manifest, it is how healings take place and all the necessary changes that we desire in our lives.

Chapter 4: Faith and The Word of God

The more the word abides in our spirits, the more our faith grows and we are enabled to do much more.

The Word of God is meant to make faith. Faith is not a theological argument, faith flows.

> ***Abstain from all appearance of evil. And the very God of peace sanctify you wholly; and I pray God your whole spirit, soul and body be preserved blameless unto the coming of our Lord Jesus Christ.*** – 1 Thessalonians 5:22-23

Your whole person—spirit, soul and body—should be of faith by believing what has been written.

A disciple abides by the Word and the Word of God also abides in Him. Fruit follows seed. See Mark 4:3-4. When the Word is sowed, it manifests in the world. Everything that God does, He does it spiritually, and it affects the natural.

> ***But the fruit of the Spirit is love, joy, peace, long suffering, kindness, goodness, faithfulness.*** – Galatians 5:22

When the Word of God abides in you, among all the other fruits that you bear is the fruit of faith. The seed of faith is the Word. He watches over His Word to perform it. He doesn't take care of us; He takes care of His Word. The entrance of God's Word brings light, light brings understanding, and thus comes faith.

CHAPTER FIVE

Faith and Your Thoughts

Your future comes out of your heart. The state of your inner being determines the boundaries to which you can go. As a man thinks in his heart, he determines the boundaries of his life. You can't think faith thoughts and not have faith results.

For as he thinks in his heart, so is he ... – Proverbs 23:7a

Old Testament terminology talks about the thinking of the heart. New Testament terminology takes about the believing of the heart.

But what does it say? "The word is near you, in your mouth and in your heart" (that is, the word of faith which we preach): – Romans 10:8

Man believes with his heart. The impact of meditation influences our thinking and believing. It is paramount that we guard our heart diligently.

> ***Keep your heart with all diligence, for out of it spring the issues of life.*** – Proverbs 4:23

Everything you see is created twice. God created, and I create. God created in the invisible realm. I create in the visible realm. The results of our thoughts manifest in the physical.

> ***A good man out of the good treasure of his heart brings forth good things, and an evil man out of the evil treasure brings forth evil things.*** – Matthew 12:35

With no Word, there will be no light. With no seed, there will be no fruit (faith), and with no faith you stay in the realm of hope. Hope is no guarantee; it is based on positive confession. Faith is the guarantee because it is the foundation of what God said.

Every event of your life is determined in the eternal realm. We have maximized the use of words for effective communication, but we have not yet maximized the use of words for creation. Whatever you see in your life has been brought forth from the eternal realm.

For every human question, God has provided the answer in the eternal realm. Faith takes the available answers from the eternal realm to the time realm. Your faith determines what time it is in your time zone.

> ***And be not conformed to this world, but be transformed by the renewing of your mind, that you may prove what is that good and acceptable and perfect will of God.*** – Romans 12:2

The Christ kind of thinking is the Word thinking. The Word

of God has the ability to transform our behavior and renew our minds. So many testimonies have been told over the years about people who stopped bad habits by studying and reading the Word. Friend, the Word of God is a double-edged sword that is able to cause any desired change in our lives.

For the word of God is living and powerful, and sharper than any two-edged sword, piercing even to the division of soul and spirit, and of joints and marrow, and is a discerner of the thoughts and intents of the heart. – Hebrews 4:12

God is omnipresent, but that doesn't mean He manifests omni-presently. God only manifests where His Word is declared.

CHAPTER SIX

Faith and Prayer

Prayer is God's empowerment mechanism. Faith is God's life mechanism. Prayer will cause my spirit to be affected by the will of God. It will enable me to know the will of God.

It is possible to agree in your spirit but not with your body. It is impossible to have a faith life without a prayer life, and it is likewise impossible to have a prayer life without a faith life.

> *And he spake a parable unto them to this end, that men ought always to pray, and not to faint; Saying, There was in a city a judge, which feared not God, neither regarded man: And there was a widow in that city; and she came unto him, saying, Avenge me of mine adversary. And he would not for a while: but afterward he said within himself, Though I fear not God, nor regard man; Yet because this widow troubleth me, I will avenge her, lest by her continual coming she weary*

> *me. And the Lord said, Hear what the unjust judge saith. And shall not God avenge his own elect, which cry day and night unto him, though he bear long with them? I tell you that he will avenge them speedily. Nevertheless when the Son of man cometh, shall he find faith on the earth?*
>
> – Luke 18:1-8 KJV

It is impossible to get results of prayer in the absence of faith, and it is also not possible to walk in faith in the absence of prayer because faith and prayer are both spiritual forces.

Prayer and the will of God

Faith begins where the will of God is known. Prayer will cause my spirit to be affected by the will of God. It will enable me to know the will of God. It is possible to agree in your spirit but not with your body.

Pray in the Holy Spirit

Praying in the Holy Spirit is praying in tongues. Through praying in the Spirit, we edify ourselves, and as a result, our faith is built up as a result. This faith that we have received must be built up by praying in the Holy Spirit.

> *But you, beloved, building up yourselves* up *on your most holy faith, praying in the Holy Spirit.* – Jude 1:20

You build yourself up by praying in tongues. Every time you do so, you are enriching your spirit man. He who speaks in tongues, his mind is unfruitful, but his spirit is built up. As we pray in tongues, *oidamen* is taking place. This is the Greek word for the writing of the Spirit on your spirit. It means "to know."

As the Spirit writes on your spirit, then you know inwardly. You have the evidence of what God is doing; God lets you in on His plans. At this point, regardless of how anyone tries to disagree with you, you can't be swayed because you know that you know.

> ***For if I pray in a tongue, my spirit prays, but my understanding is unfruitful.*** – 1 Corinthians 14:14

My spirit and my mind are different faculties. The mind connects with a physical world, while my spirit connects with the spiritual world. As the Holy Spirit makes deposit in our spirits, we speak out. The Holy Spirit in us guides what we say. If you don't say it, it will not work.

> ***For the word of God is living and powerful, and sharper than any two-edged sword, piercing even to the division of soul and spirit, and of joints and marrow, and is a discerner of the thoughts and intents of the heart.*** – Hebrews 4:12

God is omnipresent, but that doesn't mean He manifests omni-presently. God only manifests where His Word is declared.

We know not how we ought to pray

> ***Likewise the Spirit also helps in our weaknesses. For we do not know what we should pray for as we ought, but the Spirit Himself makes intercession for us with groanings which cannot be uttered.*** – Romans 8:26

Imagine you have something in particular that you want to pray for, but because the human language is so limited in vocabulary, you don't know how to express yourself in prayer in your language. Of course, inwardly, you know what you should say, but you are unable to express it.

This is how the Holy Spirit comes in to help. The Holy Spirit prays through us as we pray in tongues. He gives us the words that we should say in prayer. We are able to express ourselves according to the will of God because our prayer is from God and is circumventing our human minds. It is a spirit prayer.

Prayer is not meant to be a struggle; it should be out of faith. There is nothing that God demands from us that He has not provided. Everything that He asks from us, He has provided. He can never ask us to do what He knows we cannot do.

You have the resources. The only permanent thing in this life is what God said, so fear not. You need to stop seeking God and start ministering to Him. Feed on the Word of God. Don't stress yourself. Don't strive. Don't ask why. Don't get options. And don't try to make things happen. Don't condemn yourself. Feed on the Word. It is well.

Prayer and Fasting

Fasting is not meant to be a means to get God's attention. Most of the time, people think that when they fast, they will get God's sympathy, and He will be moved to act in their favor. This is a wrong motivation for fasting.

The purpose of fasting is to take time to fully concentrate on God. As we deny our bodies food, our spirits are able to concentrate on the Word and prayer. We are also able to hear more distinctively from Him. It is also a time that we can minister to God.

> *As they ministered to the Lord and fasted, the Holy Spirit said, "Now separate to Me Barnabas and Saul for the work to which I have called them."* – Acts 13:2

As the apostles ministered through prayer and fasting, the Holy Spirit spoke, giving them the direction that they ought to take in their ministry. The faith of the apostles was also built during this time. Later on, we read about the miracles that God performed through them and the impact that they made in the cities where they preached the gospel. They also gained the tenacity to endure all the hardships that they encountered along the way.

CHAPTER SEVEN

Possessing and Contending Aspects of Faith

Faith entails the possessing aspects and the contending aspects. To contend is to exert oneself to obtain or retain possession of. What do we contend for, and what do we possess?

Contend for the faith

Common faith is not about the Jews or the Gentiles,. It is not about age or color. It is about the one who taps into that revelation and chooses to believe. You have to contend for this faith, to make sure that the doctrine you are hearing is not watered down. Jesus said be careful how you heart.

There is a lot of stuff out there, a lot of rubbish and garbage, a lot of stuff that can't bring you to a place of faith. There is a lot of advice to be careful. Being careful is not faith. The Word of God doesn't say be careful, it says believe. When you choose to take God by His word, will most certainly be told you are risking. In the Word of God there is no risking, it is sure, it is an assurance.

> *Beloved, when I gave all diligence to write unto you of the common salvation, it was needful for me to write unto you, and exhort you that ye should earnestly contend for the faith which was once delivered unto the saints.* – Jude 1:3

Jude is concerned about a watered down and twisted doctrine that can't bring people into place of faith. His concern is that the original faith of the gospel is being destroyed by false teachers. The Word of God has one ultimate purpose; to produce faith. If the word doesn't produce faith, Jude is saying beware of this kind of doctrine. Any teaching that ultimately doesn't push you to believe, beware of it.

> *For there are certain men crept in unawares, who were before of old ordained to this condemnation, ungodly men, turning the grace of our God into lasciviousness, and denying the only Lord God, and our Lord Jesus Christ.* – Jude 1:4

He says, men will abandon the true faith, and they will be religious. Jude is concerned and calls this common salvation. In other words, it is not an exclusive salvation for a certain group of people.

It is not apartheidic or a salvation that is segregative or salvation that only belongs to the Jews. It is a common salvation that belongs to the Jews and the Gentiles alike, and it is the same salvation offered to the whole world. He says lets contend for this salvation which is the righteousness by faith.

> *Looking unto Jesus the author and finisher of our faith; who for the joy that was set before him endured the cross, despising the shame, and is set down at the right hand of the throne of God.* – Hebrews 12:2

How do you contend for the faith? You run with patience, looking unto Jesus. Faith is a spiritual force, because we are born of the Spirit, we have to be led by the Spirit and we have to be quickened by the Spirit. This puts us in a place to operate in superiority.

Faith never seeks to please men, it seeks to operate heavenly. When your faith seeks to please men, you are coming down. When your faith seeks to glorify God, you are going to the top. Religion will cause you to bow to men and kings. Faith will cause kings and men to bow to you.

Contend for the anointing

> *And it shall come to pass in that day, that his burden shall be taken away from off thy shoulder, and his yoke from off thy neck, and the yoke shall be destroyed because of the anointing.*
> – Isaiah 10:27

In the Old Testament, the common laymen; who today you would call the believers had no anointing on them, or in them. The presence of God was shut up in the Holies of Holies and only the priests had access there. God would anoint the priests, kings and prophets to operate in these respective offices.

But today, all of us can access the anointing. In the Old Testament it was not so. Today, God is anointing prophets, He's anointing kings and priests. The prophetic office includes anything that speaks for God. If you speak for God, it is prophetic, including teaching and preaching offices. Any office that is revelatory of the Word of God is prophetic.

The priesthood was about representation, for example by going into the Holy of Holies, you were representing the congregation. What we call the intercessors is what is equivalent to the priests. The problem is that the intercessors today don't fully understand what intercession is. Some think that it is spending nights in church and not eating. It is the reason our intercessors are so poor, struggling, and full of heavy burdens, because they have wrong information.

Take my yoke upon you and learn of me, for I am gentle and lowly in heart, and you will find rest for your souls. For my yoke is easy and my burden is light.
– Matthew 11:29-30

All the truth that we need to learn about the anointing is in the Word of God. We don't have to look for ten steps to being anointed. When we start looking out for formulas, that will frustrate us.

Every time you feed your spirit man with wrong information, you pay the repercussion of struggle because the anointing removes yokes, it destroys yokes. But if the yokes are being planted on you, it means there is some information you are receiving that is wrong.

How can you represent God and carry heavy burdens? It means there is something wrong. You should come to pray like a king. As we pray, there is a dispatch of the heavenly army. Faith is not apologetic; it is declarative. I believe I am a king, and I believe God is still anointing kings. Do you know why? The anointing does stuff for you without struggle. It is also able to destroy yokes.

> ***Then Jesus returned in the power of the Spirit to Galilee, and news of Him went out through all the surrounding region. And He taught in their synagogues, being glorified by all.***
> – Luke 4:14-15

Jesus returned in the power of the Holy Ghost and taught. This means that there was an anointing to teach. The anointing brought the unction to teach. You could argue that Jesus was the Son of God. This is true; Jesus was the Son of God. But He ministered on earth as a man who was anointed by God. This is different. If Jesus was ministering as the Son of God on earth, then He would not have needed the anointing. Why would the Son of God need to be anointed to teach? It doesn't make sense! If He was ministering as God in the flesh, why would He need to be anointed? Who would anoint God? Would you anoint God?

> ***... but made Himself of no reputation, taking the form of a bondservant, and coming in the likeness of men.***
> – ***Philippians*** 2:7

Right from when Mary gave birth to Him, Jesus is a Son of God. Why would He not perform miracles from when He was age 1? Why does He wait until John baptizes Him?

The Spirit of God came in bodily form, then He was anointed, then He went to the wedding in Cana and performed the first miracle. He had to be anointed for there to be miracles. John 2:11 says this was the first miracle He performed. So for Jesus to heal, He had to be anointed. But also, after He had been anointed, He had to contend for His anointing.

Satan came to Jesus and contended with him for 40 days. Why? Jesus had to contend for His power and His anointing. He submitted Himself to John the Baptist. God, in the form of Jesus, submitted Himself to a man so He could be anointed!

A few years ago, there was a man of God, and I must say I have never seen or experienced a prophet like him. He gave detailed prophecies. I submitted myself to him, carried his Bible, and washed his clothes. I served this man. I was contending for the anointing upon his life.

You need to understand that Jesus had to contend for this anointing. He laid aside all His heavenly power and submitted Himself to a man. We have to contend for this anointing. We are well able to contend because the Bible says the righteous are bold as a lion (see Proverbs 28:1).

Contend for the heritage

> *... giving thanks to the Father who has qualified us to be partakers of the inheritance of the saints in the light.*
> – Colossians 1:12

We are partakers of the divine nature. Contend for the faith, for the anointing, and the heritage. When Jesus said, ***It is finished***, at the cross, He was not talking about His assignment or His ministry. He was talking about you. He said, ***As for you, it is now finished, you can now believe.*** But for Him, He still has to forever intercede on your behalf. So it was all done for you.

> *Therefore we also, since we are surrounded by so great a cloud of witnesses, let us lay aside every weight, and the sin which so easily ensnares us, and let us run with endurance the race that is set before us, looking unto Jesus, the author and finisher of our faith, who for the joy that was set before Him endured the cross, despising the shame, and has sat down at the right hand of the throne of God.*
> – Hebrews 12:1-2

Faith will not leave anything to chance. Faith will ensure that everything we are doing is taken care of by the Word of God. We won't leave any aspect of our life to chance. We will make sure that our finances, our family, and our health is taken care of, by the Word of God, because faith will not leave anything to chance.

> *A good man leaves an inheritance to his children's children, but the wealth of the sinner is stored up for the righteous.*
> – Proverbs 13:22

The faith life ensures that you don't live an enduring life, but you live an assuring life. If you want to know when God is insulted, it is when you don't believe.

It is faith that does the praying, and grace does the healing. For demons to gain access, faith has to be absent. If faith is present, demons can't get access. When you walk in faith, demons will be clueless. Natural laws don't apply to God. If they did, God wouldn't be God.

Don't allow natural laws to be established in your thinking faculties. They are not settled in heaven. It is only the Word of God that is forever settled in heaven. Faith does not only commit to what God says, it practically expresses what God says.

CHAPTER EIGHT

Faith Is of The Now

For in it the righteousness of God is revealed from faith to faith; as it is written, "The just shall live by faith."
– Romans 1:17

I have studied the Scriptures to see if there is any other way of life, and I have failed to find a substitute for faith. Scripture says that the just shall live by faith. It is impossible for you to define faith without a corresponding manifestation. Religion tries to explain away certain truths, for example that the gifts ceased with the apostles.

Just because what you believe does not manifest, it does not mean you should start adjusting your life to explain your circumstance. Some people, after believing for a long time and not seeing the manifestation, will start to create a doctrine or a theology that suits their lifestyle. They are conformists.

And do not be conformed to this world, but be transformed by the renewing of your mind, that you may prove what is that good and acceptable and perfect will of God.
– Romans 12:2

Don't conform to the pattern that this world has set, but stick to the Word of God. It is time that the church sticks to the blueprint that is divine to the origin and intent, no matter what.

> ***By faith we understand that the worlds were framed by the word of God, so that the things which are seen were not made of things which are visible.*** *– Hebrews 11:3*

Or, I might state this passage this way: *Through faith, we understand that the supernatural put in order the natural.* Or: *Through faith, we get an illumination or understanding that the supernatural puts together the natural.* (This is my own interpretation.)

> ***"And to the angel of the church [b]of the Laodiceans write, 'These things says the Amen, the Faithful and True Witness, the Beginning of the creation of God: "I know your works, that you are neither cold nor hot. I could wish you were cold or hot. So then, because you are lukewarm, and neither cold nor hot, I will vomit you out of My mouth.***
>
> *– Revelation 3:14-16*

The Laodicean church is representative of the church age today. The church is neither hot nor cold. It is lukewarm, and all we look forward to are popcorn miracles. God, in addressing the Laodiceans, points out that their problem is that they don't have faith.

Faith has a definite course of direction. Some people say they are going to pray, and if it is God, it will come to pass. If it is not God, it will not come to pass. Now that is not faith! That is called being optimistic, and optimism does not guarantee a supernatural manifestation. God says, *I have a problem with you; you are neither hot nor cold, and you are faithless.*

I tell you that He will avenge them speedily. Nevertheless, when the Son of Man comes, will He really find faith on the earth?" – Luke 18:8

Faith has a definite position, and it will always manifest God because it has a God position. The root word for *amen* in Hebrew is **faith**. There cannot be a clear *amen* without a definite position. You can't say that God is going to heal you through chemotherapy. You determine a definite position by spiritualizing the word you receive. Thus, the *amen* says it is a final decision. (Faithful to stay in that position without being double minded).

God is faithful to His Word

So shall My word be that goes forth from My mouth; it shall not return to Me void, but it shall accomplish what I please, and it shall prosper **in the thing** *for which I sent it.*
– Isaiah 55:11

God is not faithful to you; He has no business being faithful to you. He is only faithful to Himself. If you say that God is faithful to you, you mean that He honors your word. He does not honor your word, he honors His Word. Neither does he take care of you; He takes care of His word. And that is why, despite the fact that God is a sovereign God, He only manifests where the Word of God is being declared.

Is God everywhere? Does He manifest everywhere? God is everywhere, but He manifests only where His Word is being declared. God is 100% faithful to Himself. He is not a son of man that He should lie (Numbers 23:19). The only report that is guaranteed is God's report.

In the developed countries, they have the latest health supplements that they say are guaranteed to completely heal you, but they do not. The only guaranteed supplement is the Word of God. When you 100% trust a different report, say of specialists or doctors (I seek the help of doctors, so I am not putting them down), and when you completely trust them, you are putting your trust in the hands of man, and we don't want to do that.

God has brought us from afar, and He is taking us very far. The reason you have come from afar is because you are going far. Faith is now, and as you read this book, it is coming to you.

No scripture is originally from the prophet

> *... knowing this first, that no prophecy of Scripture is of any private interpretation ...* – 2 Peter 1:20

Peter is one of the people who heard truth firsthand, so the margin of error as he preached was very small, unlike today where information has been passed down. As it is being passed on, there are many interpretations that dilute the original truth.

What Peter is saying is that no scripture is originally from the prophet; it is from God, and therefore you can't translate it according to how you understand it. The translation has to be from how God said it for there to be a manifestation. The reason why we cannot effectively interpret truth is because only God can interpret Himself.

The greatest men and women who have manifested God have been those who have the correct interpretation from how God said it. If we are going to manifest the Kingdom, we have to get the interpretation, the intent, and the mind of God at the time.

The Spirit causes us to remember

> *But the Helper, the Holy Spirit, whom the Father will send in My name, He will teach you all things, and bring to your remembrance all things that I said to you.* – John 14:26

Jesus said that the Spirit of God will bring to our remembrance all things. What He is saying is that the Spirit of God will take you to that place where that verse was being written, to what the prophet was thinking and what he saw. He causes you to experience what he experienced, what the supernatural feeling was.

The Holy Spirit will bring you to that place where Paul says that it is no longer I who lives, but Christ lives in me.

> *I have been crucified with Christ; it is no longer I who live, but Christ lives in me; and the life which I now live in the flesh I live by faith in the Son of God, who loved me and gave Himself for me.* – Galatians 2:20

What was he feeling, what was he thinking? That zeal and that commitment, power, and anointing. What gave him the confidence to make such a profound statement? The Holy Spirit will take you there, and when He takes you there, you will be able to respond the way the prophet responded, and if you respond the way the prophet responded when he received that prophecy, you will receive the same result that the prophet received when he received that prophecy. That's how revelation works.

Truth, or revelation, is progressive. If it is settled, then it is religion because the Kingdom is eternal. It cannot end. Wisdom has no measure. We only operate in that which has been revealed to us, but actually, there is more all the time. We can't finish it. It is too eternal. In your locker, there is more that is untapped.

Faith is a pathway to provision

Faith will give you what you can not buy with money. When you look at your bank account, it does not qualify. We don't have the natural ability to do the things that God puts in our hearts. When you sit down and make budgets for them, you get discouraged because we are not designed to make budgets. We are designed to call those things that be not as though they are. We are designed to call forth money.

That which is of faith cannot expire, and it cannot be taken away. If you want to miss what is called *life*, miss what is of faith.

CHAPTER NINE

Let Faith Be Your Definition

So Jesus answered and said to them, "Have faith in God ..."
– Mark 11:22

Jesus is saying to have the faith of God, referring to Genesis 1 when God created the world. There was nothing, and God said, and it was. God will demand nothing from us that is not in our ability to do. He cannot ask us to do something knowing that we have no innate ability inside us to do it. And that is why, if you have heard the voice of God to do something, it is as good as done.

The moment you hear God speak, it means something has been established eternally and is getting ready for a natural, timely manifestation. So the key is to hear the voice of God. Every human being has been designed innately with the ability to depend on God. In Genesis 3, before Satan speaks to the man, man has not yet heard any other voice. The only voice that man recognized was the voice of God. Man knew only one voice.

> ***Therefore, if anyone is in Christ, he is a new creation; old things have passed away; behold, all things have become new.***
> – 2 Corinthians 5:17

This means you have the innate ability to obey God. *Behold, old things have passed away* … it means death has passed away and life has come. It is that new life that gives us the ability to have the faith of God.

Salvation is taking man back, to hear one voice. Do you know that you are designed to hear only one voice? Why? Every other voice is a lie, including the voice of reason because it is not of eternal value. It must perish. It promises too much, and it delivers little. Before Adam heard the voice of Satan, Adam heard only one voice. God was his Source. Faith demands that God is your only Source. People promise too much and deliver too little. When God promises, He delivers.

At the new birth, this faith is birthed in your spirit as well. (You are a spirit living in a body. You are more spiritual than you are natural, and you are eternal.) Faith is not mental, it is spiritual. It is not positive confession, it is not walking on foot 20 km to go and preach. That is not faith; that is suffering. You cannot walk by faith and suffer. When the true faith starts operating in your life, you call those things that be not as though they are.

> ***For I say, through the grace given to me, to everyone who is among you, not to think of himself more highly than he ought to think, but to think soberly, as God has dealt to each one a measure of faith.*** – Romans 12:3

If you have faith, it means you are not trying to get faith.

Chapter 9: Let Faith Be Your Definition

What are you trying to do? You are trying to grow the faith God has given you and to learn how to use that faith that is inside you.

For as many as are led by the Spirit of God, they are sons of God. – Romans 8:14

The Spirit connects the life of faith into your system, so that when you begin to speak, you don't speak rubbish. You are a spirit; you only listen to the spiritual voice.

When your life gets to a place where you figure it out on your own, you are in big trouble because you are now depending on your own understanding. Cursed is the man who trusts in the arm of the flesh.

It is only the faith made available by God that we can access and walk into. It is only through faith that we can deal with mountains. And, it is only through faith that we can possess what belongs to us.

Do you know that, as faith can move mountains, doubt builds mountains? Every time you doubt, you are building a mountain. Faith does not think, faith knows. You know that you are born again. You don't need someone to explain to you. It communicates in your inner being.

It is the same with faith. Faith is like WiFi. You can't see it, and yet it has the power of connection. You reach a point where you have to faith it, until you make it. If you can consistently faith it, you will consistently make it. We can't consistently fake it, if we are to make it. Just like faith expects something, doubt also expects something.

You don't have to understand faith. You let it be stirred inside of you, and you tap into that power, so much so that nothing or no one can stop you.

I did my final exams at university when I had not studied. I simply wrote scriptures, but I graduated with an honors degree. (I am not suggesting you do the same.)

Faith cannot be emotions based. When it has an emotional foundation, that faith will be over the moment the emotions wash away. Faith must be based on the incorruptible, infallible, eternal, all powerful, alive Word of God. This is why faith can't be an experience; it is dependent on seedtime and harvest.

Stop mixing the gospel with messages like, "Be careful, you're too much," "You're praying too much," "Be careful, you have to balance." Balance what? You want to balance God? Would you rather die doubting than believing?

The testing of your faith

> ***And the Lord said, "Simon, Simon! Indeed, Satan has asked for you, that he may sift you as wheat. But I have prayed for you, that your faith should not fail; and when you have returned to Me, strengthen your brethren."*** *– Luke 22:31-32*

Faith has to be tested, but why does God test your faith? So He can locate you in His will. This is why you are tested. Jesus prayed for Peter's faith not to fail, and after he had overcome, to go in the will of God for his life, and strengthen the brethren. At Pentecost, it was Peter who stood up and preached, causing 3,000 people to receive salvation. His testing located him into the will of God.

Chapter 9: Let Faith Be Your Definition

Jesus answered them and said, "Most assuredly, I say to you, you seek Me, not because you saw the signs, but because you ate of the loaves and were filled. – John 6:26

What was the main desire that Jesus had? It was to fulfill the will of God and to finish it. God's priority is more than need oriented. Jesus was quick to recognize that the crowd that was following Him was because He had answered the need they had of food.

Yet indeed I also count all things loss for the excellence of the knowledge of Christ Jesus my Lord, for whom I have suffered the loss of all things, and count them as rubbish, that I may gain Christ and be found in Him, not having my own righteousness, which is from the law, but that which is through faith in Christ, the righteousness which is from God by faith;
– Philippians 3:8-9

Change your mind from being need oriented. The Kingdom of God is not need oriented, it is purpose oriented.

You are of a generation that is raising the standard; you are upsetting the status quo. Don't allow yourself to be defined by what you have in your hand or the money in your bank account. What you carry inside you is what defines you.

CONCLUSION

Conclusion

... whatever is not from faith is sin. – Romans 14:23

But without faith it is impossible to please Him, for he who comes to God must believe that he is, and that He is a rewarder of those who diligently seek him. – Hebrews 11:6

It is impossible for you to hear God and remain the same. God lives and operates by faith, so I am a faith man, meaning that I live and operate by faith.

In Hebrews 11:4-40 (the hall of faith), these men did different things, but they did them by faith. This was because the journey of faith is unique. The power is in our uniqueness. Don't ever try to be someone else. People will buy into your originality.

We have different kinds of faith, and therefore, our testings are different.

No temptation has overtaken you except such as is common to man; but God is faithful, who will not allow you to be tempted beyond what you are able, but with the temptation will also make the way of escape, that you may be able to bear it.
– 1 Corinthians 10:13

Whatever challenge comes to you is yours alone. You are unique. Before you trust God for a physical victory, ensure you have a spiritual victory. It is impossible to apply God if you don't apply faith. God believes that whatever happens to me, I am well able to handle it.

> ***Then Peter opened his mouth and said: "In truth I perceive that God shows no partiality…"*** – Acts 10:34

At whatever level you are, greater can happen at any time. There is nothing wrong with you being in a difficult situation. What is wrong is you being in that situation and believing that you are not an overcomer. You believe you are different from the great men of this world. But having been born of incorruptible seed is what makes you great.

Faith doesn't wait for good things to come to you; faith brings forth good things out of you. In the short run, faith looks foolish, but in the long run, doubt is eternally foolish.

A CALL TO SALVATION

A Call To Salvation

But what does it say? "The word is near you, in your mouth and in your heart" (that is, the word of faith which we preach): that if you confess with your mouth the Lord Jesus and believe in your heart that God has raised Him from the dead, you will be saved. – Romans 10:8-9

This may sound like a cliché, but allow me to add my voice to the thousands who have said it: *Receiving Jesus as your personal Lord and Savior is the best decision that you can ever make in your life.*

Read loudly the prayer below:

Lord Jesus, I give You my life that You may give me everlasting life. I repent of my sins, and I ask You to wash me clean and white with Your precious blood. Come into my heart. I make You my Lord and Savior.

In Jesus' name, Amen.

If you prayed this prayer, we believe that you have been born again. Please find a Bible-believing church and ask to be baptized in water.

We would also like to hear from you. Send us an email to:

henrykatabazi@gmail.com

About The Author

HENRY BYAMUKAMA

Henry Byamukama is the Lead Pastor of Breakthrough Life Church, Uganda, and the FaithLife Fellowship, a weekly gathering of believers hungry for the Word of God.

Pastor Henry's life changed the day he received the revelation of faith. He has been preaching and teaching about faith for near two decades in churches around the world. He currently operates out of Uganda and the United States.

Henry is married to Lillian, and they have two wonderful children, Hadassah and Corban, as well as an ever-expanding family of spiritual children.

www.ingramcontent.com/pod-product-compliance
Lightning Source LLC
Chambersburg PA
CBHW070549090426
42735CB00013B/3117